This book belongs to

_____

_____

For Sebastian, Daniel and Davina L.R.

For Gabriel A.W.

Best-Loved Prayers

Treasures for a lifetime

Compiled by Lois Rock

Illustrations by Alison Wisenfeld

Tommy
NELSON

Thomas Nelson, Inc.
Nashville

Compilation by Lois Rock
Copyright © 1996 Lion Publishing
Illustrations © 1996 Alison Wisenfeld
All rights reserved

First North American Edition
Published 1998 by Tommy Nelson™,
a division of Thomas Nelson, Inc.,
Nashville, Tennessee.
ISBN 0-8499-5819-9

Acknowledgments
Every effort has been made to trace and contact copyright owners. If there are
any inadvertent omissions or errors in the acknowledgments, we apologize to
those concerned and will remedy these in the next edition.

"Let our friendships be strong, O Lord . . ." by Rt Rev. Christopher Herbert,
taken from *Laughter, Silence and Shouting*, edited by Kathy Keay, published by
Marshall Pickering, reproduced with permission.

A catalog record for this book is available
from the British Library

98 99 00 01 02 Book Print 9 8 7 6 5 4 3 2 1

Printed and bound in Spain

About prayer

Prayer is spending time with God: talking, listening, learning, loving, laughing and crying together.

But how can anyone pray if they don't know God?

One way to start is to use prayers written by people who know God as a friend. This book is a collection of some of the best-loved.

Some of these prayers were written a long time ago. They use words and expressions that were common then but are not so now. Some are very simple. Others are written in the form of a poem.

Try reading them thoughtfully. You may well find that the prayers talk about things that matter to you—your hopes and fears, your joys and sorrows. Even more, you may begin to see how the writers think God can help with those things.

With the prayers are words from the Bible, the special book of the Christian faith, which tell you even more about what people believe God is like and about how much God loves people and longs to be their friend.

When a person begins to see that God is indeed kind and gentle and welcoming, they find it easier to say their own special prayers to God. Then they are likely to say everyday prayers in everyday words.

And they can find out what God says and does in answer.

God is the maker of the world

For flowers that bloom about our feet,
Father, we thank thee.
For tender grass so fresh, so sweet,
Father, we thank thee.
For song of bird and hum of bee,
For all things fair we hear or see,
Father in heaven, we thank thee.

For blue of stream and blue of sky,
Father, we thank thee.
For pleasant shade of branches high,
Father, we thank thee.
For fragrant air and cooling breeze,
For the beauty of the blooming trees,
Father in heaven, we thank thee.

For this new morning with its light,
Father, we thank thee.
For rest and shelter of the night,
Father, we thank thee.
For health and food, for love and friends,
For everything thy goodness sends,
Father in heaven, we thank thee.

Ralph Waldo Emerson (1803–82)

The world and all that is
in it belong to the Lord.

From the book of Psalms

God cares for the world

Dear Father, hear and bless
Thy beasts and singing birds;
And guard with tenderness
Small things that have no words.

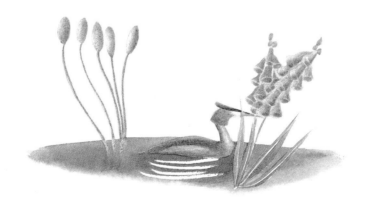

Jesus said, "Not one sparrow is
forgotten by God."

From Luke's Gospel

God cares for me

Dear Father who hast all things made,
And carest for them all,
There's none too great for your great love,
Nor anything too small.
If you can spend such tender care
On things that grow so wild,
How wonderful your love must be
For me, your little child.

G. W. Briggs (1875–1959)

Jesus said, "God takes care of the birds.
And you are worth so much more than
the birds."

From Luke's Gospel

God provides all we need

The bread is pure and fresh,
The water is cool and clear.
Lord of all life, be with us,
Lord of all life, be near.

A prayer from Africa

Jesus said, "I am the bread of life . . .
The person who comes to me will
never be hungry . . . the person who
believes in me will never be
thirsty."

From John's Gospel

God comes to us in the person Jesus

Thou didst leave thy throne and thy kingly crown
When thou camest to earth for me;
But in Bethlehem's home was there found no room
For thy holy Nativity:
O come to my heart, Lord Jesus;
There is room in my heart for thee.

Emily E. S. Elliott

The angel Gabriel came to a girl named Mary and said, "You will give birth to a son and you will name him Jesus. He will be called the Son of God."

From Luke's Gospel

God welcomes children

Jesus, friend of little children,
Be a friend to me;
Take my hand and ever keep me
Close to thee.

Never leave me, nor forsake me,
Ever be my friend;
For I need thee from life's dawning
To its end.

Jesus called the children to him and said, "Let the children come to me and do not stop them . . ."

From Luke's Gospel

God takes good care of those who follow him

Loving Shepherd of thy sheep,
Keep thy lamb in safety keep;
Nothing can thy power withstand,
None can pluck me from thy hand.

Jesus said, "I am the good shepherd. My sheep are the people who follow me. I am willing to die to keep them safe."

From John's Gospel

God is a loving father

Our Father which art in heaven,
Hallowed be thy Name,
Thy kingdom come,
Thy will be done,
in earth as it is in heaven.
Give us this day our daily bread.
And forgive us our trespasses,
As we forgive them that trespass against us;
And lead us not into temptation;
But deliver us from evil.

From the Gospels by Matthew and Luke

For thine is the kingdom,
The power and the glory,
For ever and ever. Amen.

An ancient ending for the prayer
Jesus taught

One of Jesus' followers said,
"Lord, teach us to pray."
Jesus gave them
this prayer.

From Luke's Gospel

God is the very best parent

O God,
as truly as you are our father,
so just as truly you are our mother.
We thank you, God our father,
for your strength and goodness.
We thank you, God our mother,
for the closeness of your caring.
O God, we thank you for the great love
you have for each one of us.

Julian of Norwich

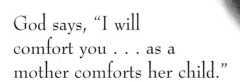

God says, "I will
comfort you . . . as a
mother comforts her child."

From the book of Isaiah

God is ready to forgive

Dear Lord and Father of mankind,
Forgive our foolish ways!
Reclothe us in our rightful mind,
In purer lives your service find,
In deeper reverence praise.

J. G. Whittier (1807–92)

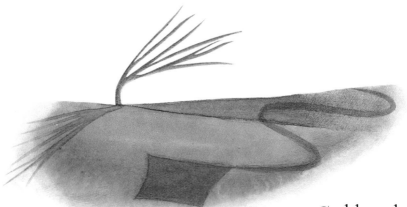

God has shown us love and
kindness. God's Holy Spirit washes
us clean from all we used to do that was foolish and
wrong, and gives us new life.

From Paul's letter to Titus

God gives us a new start . . . a new life

Christ is now risen again
From his death and all his pain:
Therefore will we merry be,
And rejoice with him gladly.
Kyrieleison.
Had he not risen again,
We had been lost, this is plain:
But since he is risen in deed,
Let us love him all with speed.
Kyrieleison.
Now is a time of gladness,
To sing of the Lord's goodness:
Therefore glad now will we be,
And rejoice in him only.
Kyrieleison.

Miles Coverdale (1488–1568)

Kyrieleison (usually *Kyrie eleison*)
is Greek for the prayer
"Lord, have mercy."

God raised Jesus Christ
from death.
And God gives you new life with Jesus.

From Paul's letter to the Colossians

God helps us be the people we long to be

God be in my head, and in my
understanding;
God be in my eyes, and in my looking;
God be in my mouth, and in my speaking;
God be in my heart, and in my thinking;
God be at my end and at my departing.

From a Book of Hours (1514)

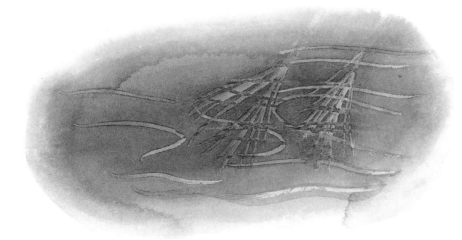

My dear friends, we are
now God's children . . .
and we have God's
nature in us.

**From the first letter
of John**

God helps us to love one another

 Let our friendships be strong, O Lord,
that they become a blessing to others . . .
Let our friendships be open, O Lord,
that they may be a haven for others . . .
Let our friendships be gentle, O Lord,
that they may bring peace to others . . .
for Jesus' sake. Amen.

C. Herbert

Dear friends, let us love one another,
because love comes from God.

From the first letter of John

God listens when we pray for others

Keep watch, dear Lord, with those who work, or watch, or weep this night, and give your angels charge over those who sleep.

Tend the sick, Lord Christ; give rest to the weary, bless the dying, soothe the suffering, pity the afflicted, shield the joyous; and all for your love's sake.

Saint Augustine (354–430)

God heals the broken-hearted and bandages their wounds.

From the book of Psalms

God takes care of all the things we worry about

We commend unto you, O Lord,
our souls and our bodies,
our minds and our thoughts,
our prayers and our hopes,
our health and our work,
our life and our death,
our parents and brothers and sisters,
our benefactors and friends,
our neighbors, our countrymen,
and all Christian folk,
this day and always.

Lancelot Andrewes (1555–1626)

Leave all your worries with God,
because God cares for you.

From the first letter of Peter

God is our guide

My dearest Lord,
Be thou a bright flame before me,
Be thou a guiding star above me,
Be thou a smooth path beneath me,
Be thou a kindly shepherd behind me,
Today and for evermore.

Saint Colomba (521–597)

God says, "I will teach you the
way you should go."

From the book of Psalms

God can be trusted

Thy way, not mine, O Lord,
However dark it be;
Lead me by thine own hand,
Choose out the path for me.

Horatio Bonar

God will take you through hard times . . .
but God will stay close . . .
and you will hear God's voice behind you saying,
"Here is the path. Follow it."

From the book of Isaiah

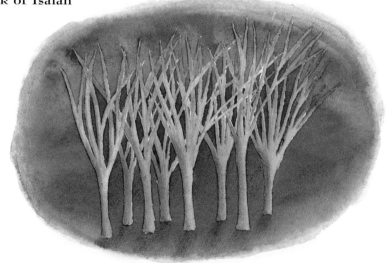

God protects us

Protect me, O Lord;
My boat is so small,
And your sea is so big.

Traditional Breton Prayer

Jesus stood up in the storm-tossed boat.
"Be quiet," he commanded the wind.
To the waves he said, "Be still."
And there was a great calm.

From Mark's Gospel

God watches over each one of us

Lord, keep us safe this night,
Secure from all our fears;
May angels guard us while we sleep,
Till morning light appears.

John Leland (1754–1841)

The angel said, "God loves you, so don't
let anything worry you or frighten you."

From the book of Daniel

God looks after those who travel far away

May the road rise to meet you.
May the wind be always at your back.
May the sun shine warm upon your face.
May the rains fall softly upon your fields.
Until we meet again,
May God hold you in the hollow of his hand.

Traditional blessing from Ireland

Jesus said, "I will be with you always,
to the end of the age."

From Matthew's Gospel

Going further . . .

Below is a list of references so that you can look up the words and sayings which have been taken from the Bible. The title of the page where the Bible saying appears is followed by the name of the book of the Bible, the chapter number and the verse number.

God is the maker of the world *Psalm 24:1*

God cares for the world *Luke 12:6*

God cares for me *Luke 12:24*

God provides all we need *John 6:35*

God comes to us in the person Jesus *Luke 1:26–32*

God welcomes children *Luke 18:16*

God takes good care of those who follow him *John 10:11–15*

God is a loving father *Luke 11:1–4; Matthew 6:9–13*

God is the very best parent *Isaiah 66:13*

God is ready to forgive *Titus 3:3–5*

God gives us a new start . . . a new life *Colossians 2:12–13*

God helps us be the people we long to be *1 John 3:2, 9*

God helps us to love one another *1 John 4:7*

God listens when we pray for others *Psalm 147:3*

God takes care of all the things we worry about *1 Peter 5:7*

God is our guide *Psalm 32:8*

God can be trusted *Isaiah 30:20–21*

God protects us *Mark 4:35–39*

God watches over each one of us *Daniel 10:18*

God looks after those who travel far away *Matthew 28:20*